HOW-TO LIBRARY

LEARNING TO KNIT

WITHDRAWN

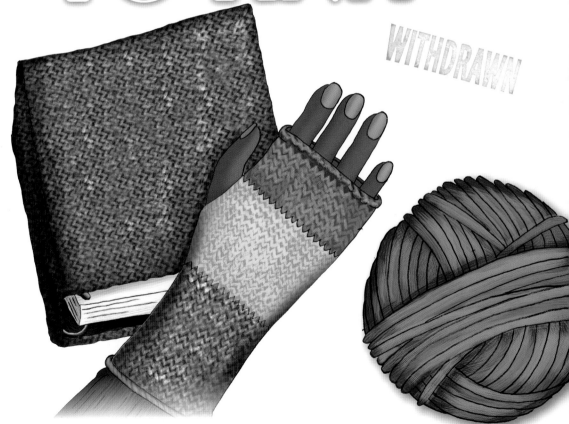

By Dana Meachen Rau • Illustrated by Kathleen Petelinsek

CHERRY LAKE PUBLISHING • ANN ARBOR, MICHIGAN

A NOTE TO ADULTS:
Please review the instructions for these craft projects before your children make them. Be sure to help them with any crafts you do not think they can safely conduct on their own.

A NOTE TO KIDS:
Be sure to ask an adult for help with these craft activities when you need it. Always put your safety first!

Published in the United States of America by Cherry Lake Publishing
Ann Arbor, Michigan
www.cherrylakepublishing.com

Content Adviser: Dr. Julia L. Hovanec, Professor of Art Education, Kutztown University, Kutztown, Pennsylvania

Photo Credits: Page 4, ©Shebeko/Shutterstock, Inc.; page 5, ©Bright/Dreamstime.com; page 6, ©Le Do/Shutterstock, Inc.; page 7, ©Robnroll/Shutterstock, Inc.; page 8, ©oksix/Shutterstock, Inc.; pages 23, 24, 25, 26, and 28, ©Dana Meachen Rau; page 29, ©Shrewsbury Design and Photography/Shutterstock, Inc.; page 32, ©Tania McNaboe

Library of Congress Cataloging-in-Publication Data
Rau, Dana Meachen, 1971–
  Learning to knit / by Dana Meachen Rau.
    pages cm — (How-to library. Crafts)
  Includes bibliographical references and index.
  ISBN 978-1-61080-477-6 (lib. bdg.) —
ISBN 978-1-61080-564-3 (e-book) — ISBN 978-1-61080-651-0 (pbk.)
1. Knitting—Juvenile literature. I. Title.
  TT820.R375 2012
  677'.028245—dc23   2012002127

Cherry Lake Publishing would like to acknowledge the work of The Partnership for 21st Century Skills. Please visit www.21stcenturyskills.org for more information.

Printed in the United States of America
Corporate Graphics Inc.
July 2012
CLFA11

HOW-TO LIBRARY

TABLE OF CONTENTS

Creating with Yarn

Yarn comes in a wide variety of colors.

Do you love to create things? An artist makes art with paint or clay. A builder uses bricks and wood to make a house. Chefs make meals from a kitchen full of ingredients. Knitters use yarn to make cozy clothing and stylish accessories.

Knitting is a hobby for all kinds of people. If you are the kind of person who likes to sit and be quiet, knitting can be relaxing. If you are always on the go, knitting is a good project to toss in a bag and bring along.

Knitting is the act of making loops of yarn with long needles. Using just two types of stitches, a knitter can turn a simple strand of yarn into mittens, scarves, bags, sweaters, socks, or pillows.

Give knitting a try. You can knit on your own or with friends. You may have an older family member who likes to knit, too. Spend time together sharing ideas and supplies. Some towns even have knitting clubs for kids, teens, and adults.

You'll be amazed at all the unique items you can create with yarn.

You can make almost any kind of clothing out of yarn.

Spread the Word

People have been knitting sweaters for hundreds of years.

Historians learn about the past by looking at **artifacts**. Artifacts are objects or pieces of objects from long ago. Items made of stone, pottery, or metal can last a long time. But **textiles** don't last very long. So there aren't many knitted objects from far in the past for people to study.

But a few textile artifacts do remain. If you go to a textile museum, you might see socks from Egypt that are more than 1,000 years old. Some historians believe that knitting began in the Arab world. When Europeans explored and traded with these people, they may have learned knitting skills that they brought back to their own countries.

Knitting skills spread around the world. Knitters made socks, hats, mittens, stockings, sweaters, bags, lace, and toys. People around the world used different stitches, patterns, and colors. They based their designs on the materials and traditions of their home countries.

You can carry on the long tradition of knitting today. Make items to wear. Or make items for fun. Spread the word to your friends and start a knitting group. With just two needles, some yarn, and some basic stitches, you'll be ready to create!

It only takes a few basic supplies to get started with your own knitting projects.

Choosing Your Yarn

You'll be amazed at the selection of colors and patterns offered at yarn stores.

In a yarn store, you'll see bins and shelves running wall to wall and floor to ceiling. These colorful displays hold **skeins** of yarn (also sometimes called balls or **hanks**). If you don't have a yarn store in your area, craft and hobby stores may sell yarn. So which yarn do you choose?

DYE LOTS

A number stamped on the yarn's label tells you the dye lot. If you need to buy more than one skein of the same color, try to buy ones with the same number. Because they were dyed in the same batch, the color will match best.

Type of Yarn

Yarn can be made from natural or **synthetic** fibers. Some natural fibers come from animals, such as wool (sheep), angora (rabbits), mohair (goats), and silk (silkworms). Cotton, linen, and bamboo yarns come from plant fibers. Synthetic fibers are man-made. These include acrylic, nylon, or polyester. Some yarns are a blend of natural and synthetic fibers.

Weight of Yarn

Weight is the thickness of the yarn. It ranges from extra fine to super bulky. A knitter might use fine yarn to knit socks. Bulky yarn is good for an extra-warm scarf. Beginners should start with a medium weight yarn, also called **worsted** yarn.

Texture and Color

Yarns have many different **textures**. Some are soft, bumpy, or even rough. Novelty yarns might have pom-poms or glitter attached to them. Some even look like feathers or ribbons.

You'll have a rainbow of colors to choose from. Some yarns are solid colors. Others are a mix of colors. These yarns can give your fabric a tie-dyed or striped pattern.

Price

Yarn comes in a range of prices. Think of your project and your budget. If you are making a large object such as a blanket, you may want to choose a less expensive yarn. But if you only need one skein, you might want to splurge on an expensive yarn.

Basic Tools

You need needles to get started. Needles have different number measurements. Thicker needles have higher numbers. Needles can be made from metal, plastic, bamboo, or wood.

Knitters use a few different kinds of needles in their projects:

- *Straight needles* come in pairs. One end of a straight needle is pointed, so it can pick up stitches. The other end has a wide knob that keeps the stitch from sliding off. Straight needles are used to create flat pieces of fabric by stitching back and forth in rows.
- *Circular needles* are made of two pointed needles connected by a plastic cord. They are used to create tubes of fabric.
- *Double-pointed needles* are for more advanced knitters. Both ends of a double-pointed needle look like the pointed side of a straight needle. They are used for knitting tubes.

You'll also need these tools in your knitting bag:

- *Scissors*—A small, sharp pair is perfect for cutting yarn.
- *Tape measure*—This flexible ruler makes it easy to measure yarn and fabric.
- *Paper and pencil*—These are helpful for keeping track of stitches and rows, or for marking your place on a pattern.
- *Yarn needle*—This looks like a sewing needle, but it's not sharp and it has a larger **eye**. You'll use it to sew in the ends of yarn when you finish a project or sew together pieces of knitted fabric.
- *Straight pins*—These will help you mark and count stitches.
- *Crochet needle*—This is a thick needle with a hook at the end to help you pick up missed stitches.

KNITTING TO GO

Store your knitting in a bag to keep the balls from rolling around the floor, and to make sure you don't lose your tools or patterns. If you want to bring your knitting along on a trip, you can just grab your bag and go.

Getting Started

Slipknot, step one

The first step to knitting is **casting on** stitches.

To Make a Slipknot

Your yarn has two ends—the tail yarn
(the cut end of the yarn) and the ball yarn
(the yarn that leads to the ball).

1. Pull a piece of yarn from the ball and
   make a loop about 12 inches (30.5
   centimeters) from the tail. Slip one
   of your needles into the loop and
   use it to pull the ball yarn through
   the loop.
2. Pull gently on both yarn ends to
   tighten the knot onto the needle.

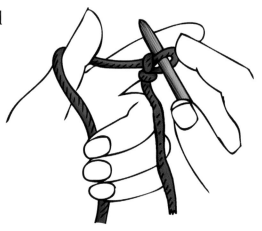

Slipknot, step two

To Cast On Stitches

1. Hold the needle with the slipknot
   in one hand. Place the yarn over
   the thumb of your other hand,
   with the ball yarn hanging down.
   Pick up the ball yarn with the
   tip of the needle.

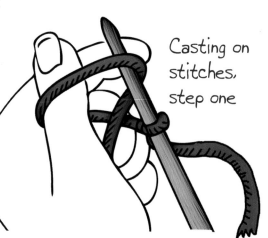

Casting on
stitches,
step one

2. Pull the ball yarn tight. You now have a stitch. Repeat again and again to make more stitches. Keep practicing until it feels comfortable.

Casting on stitches, step two

HAVE A BALL
A hank is a loop of yarn folded and twisted together. If you buy a hank, you'll have to make it into a ball before you start knitting.

Untwist the hank and keep the large loops of yarn together. Ask a friend to put out her hands. Place the loops between them. (You can also use the back of a chair.) Wind the tail end of the yarn around your fingers about ten times. Then take the loops off your fingers and start winding the yarn in the other direction so a ball starts to form. Continue winding the yarn around your ball turning the ball now and then. Your friend (or the chair) will keep the yarn from getting tangled.

Knit Stitch

The knit stitch makes a loop that forms a V shape in the fabric. Here's how to do it:

1. Cast on a row of stitches. Hold the needle with the cast on stitches in your left hand pointing right. Hold the empty needle in your right hand pointing left. As you work, you'll be moving the stitches from the left-hand needle to the right-hand needle.

2. Slide the tip of the right-hand needle into the bottom of the first stitch of the left-hand needle. Form an X with the needles. The right-hand needle should be behind the left one.

3. Holding the needles together with your left hand, use your right hand to wind the yarn counterclockwise around the tip of the right-hand needle.

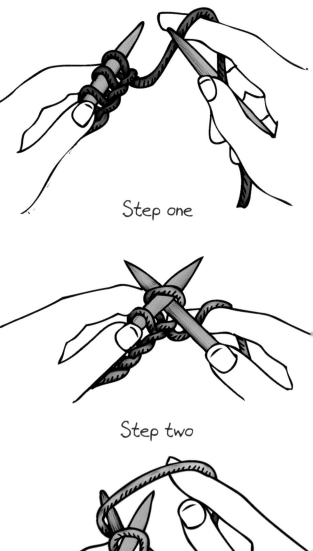

Step one

Step two

Step three

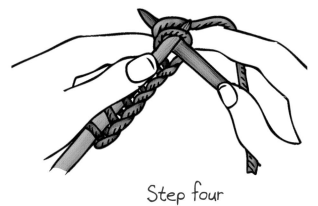

Step four

Step four

Step five

4. Slide the tip of the right-hand needle down through the stitch, bringing the new loop of yarn downward, too. Slide it off the tip of the left-hand needle.

5. Now you have a new stitch on the right-hand needle.

6. Continue across all of the stitches until the new stitches are all on the right-hand needle. You have completed a row of knit stitches!

7. To start the next row, switch the needles so that your left hand is holding the one with the stitches and your right hand holds the empty one.

Purl Stitch

The purl stitch creates a small bump in the fabric. Here's how to do it:

1. Slide the tip of the right-hand needle into the top of the first stitch of the left-hand needle. Form an X with the needles. The right-hand needle should be in front of the left one.
2. Use your right hand to wind the yarn counterclockwise around the tip of the right-hand needle.

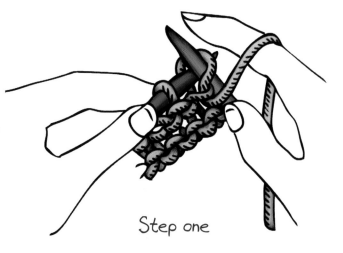

Step one

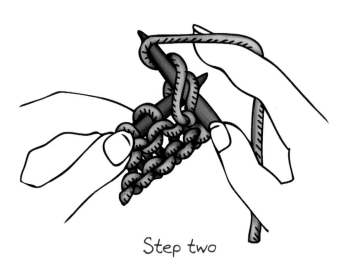

Step two

Step three

Step four

3. Slide the tip of the right-hand needle up through the stitch, bringing the new loop of yarn upward, too. Slide it off the tip of the left-hand needle.

4. Now you have a new stitch on the right-hand needle.

5. Continue across all of the stitches until the new stitches are all on the right-hand needle. You have completed a row of purl stitches!

6. To start the next row, switch the needles so that your left hand is holding the one with the stitches and your right hand holds the empty one.

STITCH OPPOSITES
A purl stitch is just the opposite of a knit stitch. If you look at the back of a purl stitch, it looks like a knit stitch. If you look at the back of a knit stitch, it looks like a purl.

Reaching the End

Once you have finished a piece of fabric, you need to get the stitches off the needles without unraveling your work. **Binding off** creates a line of final stitches to hold your fabric together. Always work loosely when you bind off.

To Bind Off

1. Knit the first two stitches onto the right-hand needle. With your left-hand needle, lift stitch A over stitch B and off the end of the right-hand needle. You'll have one stitch left on the right-hand needle.

2. Knit the next stitch onto the right-hand needle. Again, lift stitch A over stitch B and off the end. Continue across all of the stitches in the row until you just have one stitch on the right-hand needle.

3. Pull open this last stitch to make a big loop. Pull the yarn through the loop and then pull the loop tight. Cut off the yarn, leaving about a 12-inch (30.5 cm) tail. Now you have a yarn tail at both the start of your piece, where you cast on stitches, and at the end of the piece, where you bound off.

To Tuck in the Loose Ends
1. Thread the cast on yarn tail onto a yarn needle.
2. Weave it in and out of the stitches of the closest row on the back of your piece.
3. Pull off the yarn needle and trim the yarn close to the work.
4. Repeat with the bound off yarn tail.

MAKING MISTAKES

As you work, it's a good idea to count the stitches on the needle every few rows. You may find you have more or less of what you started with. This means that you either created a new stitch or dropped a stitch by mistake.

Look closely at each row of knitting to find your mistake. Carefully slip out the needles and unravel your work up to your mistake. Then slip the needles back on and rework from there. Or you can use a crochet needle to grab a missed stitch and pull it back through the loop and onto the knitting needle.

Swatch Out!

Different combinations of knit stitches and purl stitches create different looks.

Garter stitch

Garter Stitch: If you knit every row, you will get an overall bumpy look on the front and back of the fabric.

Stockinette Stitch: If you knit a row, then purl a row, and continue **alternating** rows, you will get a flat side (all V shapes) on the front and all bumps on the back.

Stickinette stitch

Before you start any knitting project, it's good to make a **swatch**. This small piece of knitted fabric (usually about 4 inches (10 cm) square) can help you test what size needle is best for the yarn and for your own personal knitting style.

A swatch also allows you to test the **gauge** of the yarn. Gauge is the number of stitches and rows per inch of knitted fabric. The yarn label usually lists its gauge with a specific needle (such as 5 stitches = 1 inch (2.5 cm) on US 11 (8 millimeter) needles). A pattern will also tell you the project's gauge.

How to Make a Swatch

1. Look at the pattern to see what the gauge needs to be. For example: Gauge: 18 stitches and 24 rows = 4 inches (10 cm) in stockinette stitch using US 8 (5 mm) needles

2. This pattern calls for 18 stitches. So cast on the 18, plus 4 more. The extra stitches will make it easier to check the gauge.

3. Knit or purl as needed across the desired number of rows. In this case, it is stockinette stitch, so you alternate knit and purl rows until you knit 24 rows. Then continue for 4 more rows.

4. Bind off loosely.

5. Lay your piece flat. In the middle of the work (not too close to the edges), measure 4 inches (10 cm) across and mark with pins. Then measure 4 inches (10 cm) up and down and mark with pins. Count the stitches and rows within the pins. Does it match the gauge of the pattern?

If your piece is smaller than the gauge, you are a tight knitter. You might want to use bigger needles to get the right size. If your piece is larger than the gauge, you are a loose knitter. You may need to go down a needle size.

Sample swatch

PATTERN ABBREVIATIONS
When you read a pattern, you'll notice that knitters use abbreviations for common knitting terms. You may come across these abbreviations in knitting books:

BO	bind off
CO	cast on
WS	wrong side
RS	right side
k	knit
p	purl
st(s)	stitches
st st	stockinette stitch

21

Bold Stripe Hand Warmers

When the weather gets cold, nothing keeps you toastier than knitted hugs for your hands.

Materials

1 skein worsted weight yarn of Color 1
1 skein worsted weight yarn of Color 2
1 skein worsted weight yarn of Color 3
Size US 8 (5 mm) straight needles (or correct size to match gauge)
Yarn needle
Scissors

Gauge

18 stitches and 24 rows = 4 inches (10 cm) in stockinette stitch using US 8 (5 mm) needles

Steps

1. Cast on 30 stitches of Color 1. Leave a 12-inch (30.5 cm) tail of cast on yarn.
2. Work in stockinette stitch for 20 rows.
3. Change to Color 2 by tying Color 2 to Color 1 at the beginning of a row with a small knot.

4. Work in stockinette stitch for 10 rows with Color 2.
5. Change to Color 3. Work in stockinette stitch for 10 rows with Color 3.
6. Bind off loosely. You will have a rectangle of fabric.
7. Fold the rectangle in half with right sides facing. Line up the edges. Thread the cast on tail of Color 1 (in the bottom corner) through the yarn needle. Sew up the side of the rectangle by threading through a stitch on one side, then the other, back and forth up the seam. When you reach Color 2, sew an extra stitch, knot the yarn, and weave in the end.
8. Use the bind off tail of Color 3 (in top corner) to sew the seam of Color 3. Knot the yarn and weave in the end. Do not sew the seam of Color 2—that's the thumbhole.
9. Weave in all the ends of loose yarn and snip off the extra yarn. Turn your hand warmer right-side out.
10. Repeat all the steps to make a matching hand warmer.

TYPES OF STRIPES

Use this basic pattern to make different types of striped hand warmers. You can make the stripes all the same size. Or you can make some big and some small. If you have a lot of scrap yarn, try making each row a different stripe. Sketch out some ideas on graph paper before you start knitting, to see what you like best.

Double Color Binder Cover

This two-colored cover will give your binder a whole new look.

In this project, you'll pair two yarns together to make a thick, multicolored cover to wrap around your binder. Be extra careful to pick up both yarns with each stitch.

Materials

2 skeins worsted weight yarn of Color 1
2 skeins worsted weight yarn of Color 2
Size US 11 (8 mm) straight needles (or correct size to match gauge)
Tape measure
Scissors
Yarn needle
1-inch loose-leaf binder

Gauge

11 stitches and 16 rows = 4 inches
   (10 cm) in stockinette stitch using
   US 8 (5 mm) needles

Steps

1. Knit with Color 1 and Color 2 yarns together as if they were one strand of yarn. Cast on 35 stitches.

2. Work in stockinette stitch (knit one row, purl one row, repeat) for 175 rows, until the piece measures about 44 inches (112 cm).

3. Bind off loosely.

4. Fold over one end of the fabric about 10 inches (25 cm), right sides together. With the yarn needle, sew up the two sides. Repeat on the other end of the fabric. Weave in all of the ends on the wrong side of the fabric.

5. Turn the end "pockets" right-side out.

6. Slide the side pockets over each side of your binder.

Floor Flair
T-Shirt Rug

This rug is a great way to make use of your old T-shirts.

Yarn isn't the only material you can use for knitting. This project is a good way to reuse T-shirts that don't fit or are too worn out to wear. Add a little flair to your floor with this striped rug.

Materials
8 to 10 old T-shirts in various colors
Scissors
Size US 15 (10 mm) straight needles
   (or correct size to match gauge)
Yarn needle

Gauge

9 stitches and 14 rows = 4 inches (10 cm) in garter stitch using US 8 (5 mm) needles

Finished rug equals 18 x 24 inches (46 x 61 cm).

Steps

1. Cut off the hem of a T-shirt and **discard** it.
2. Starting at the bottom of the shirt, cut the fabric around and around into one continuous 1-inch (2.5 cm) strip until you reach the armholes.
3. Cut off both of the arms and discard them.
4. Continue cutting a strip around the fabric until you reach the neck hole. Discard the neck trim.
5. Repeat with the rest of the T-shirts.

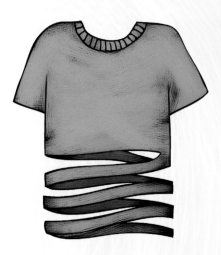

Make sure your strip stays about the same width all the way around.

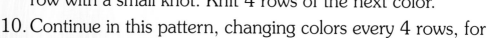

6. Wind up the strips into balls of T-shirt "yarn."

7. Cast on 40 stitches, starting with any color you wish.

8. Work in garter stitch (knit every row) for 4 rows.

9. Change to another color by tying the next T-shirt yarn to the first at the beginning of a row with a small knot. Knit 4 rows of the next color.

10. Continue in this pattern, changing colors every 4 rows, for 84 rows.

11. Bind off loosely.

12. With a yarn needle, weave in all the loose ends of yarn into the back side of the rug.

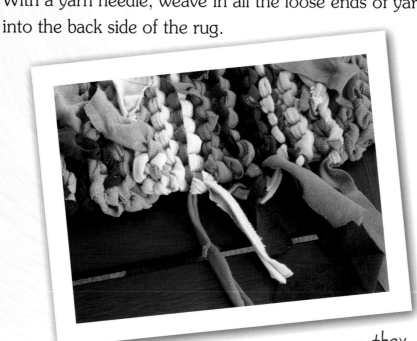

Weave the loose ends into your rug so they don't hang off the sides.

Practice and Experiment

Knitting takes a lot of practice. You may get frustrated if the yarn gets knotted, your piece unravels, or your needle slips out of the stitches. Don't give up. Try again. When your hands get used to the motion of knitting, you'll be able to work faster and make fewer mistakes. Remember, even advanced knitters mess up sometimes.

Mistakes aren't always a bad thing. You don't always have to follow a pattern. Experiment with different yarns and needle sizes. For example, try knitting with a fine yarn with big needles. Or mix a few different novelty yarns together. Swatches are small and easy to knit. When you have lots of swatches, sew them together to make a crazy quilt!

You can knit beautiful blankets that will keep you warm in the winter.

Glossary

alternating (AWL-tur-nay-ting) going back and forth between two things

artifacts (AHR-tuh-fakts) objects made or changed by human beings

binding off (BINE-ding AWF) removing stitches from a needle so they don't unravel

casting on (KAS-ting AHN) placing the first row of stitches onto a needle

discard (dis-KAHRD) throw away

eye (EYE) the hole at one end of a sewing needle

gauge (GAYJ) a measurement of the number of stitches and rows per inch of knitted fabric

hanks (HANGKS) loops of yarn folded and twisted together

skeins (SKEYNZ) lengths or bundles of yarn

swatch (SWATCH) a small sample of fabric

synthetic (sin-THET-ik) man-made

textiles (TEK-stihlz) woven or knitted fabrics or cloths

textures (TEKS-churz) the different ways things feel

worsted (WURS-tid) medium weight

For More Information

Books

Blanchette, Peg, and Terri Thibault. *12 Easy Knitting Projects.* Nashville, TN: Williamson Books, 2006.

Guy, Lucinda, and François Hall. *Kids Learn to Knit.* North Pomfret, VT: Trafalgar Square Publishing, 2006.

Platt, Richard. *They Wore What?! The Weird History of Fashion and Beauty.* Minnetonka, MN: Two-Can, 2007.

Sadler, Judy Ann. *Quick Knits.* Toronto, ON: Kids Can Press, 2006.

Web Sites

Craft Yarn Council: Top 10 Yarn Questions & Answers

www.craftyarncouncil.com/top10qa.html

Learn more about different types of yarn.

The Textile Museum

www.textilemuseum.org

Look at photos of famous artwork to get ideas for your own projects.

Victoria and Albert Museum: Knitting

www.vam.ac.uk/page/k/knitting

Check out the creations of expert knitters.

Index

About the Author

Dana Meachen Rau is the author of more than
300 books for children on many topics, including
science, history, cooking, and crafts. She creates,
experiments, researches, and writes from her home
office in Burlington, Connecticut.